deutsch | englisch

Welterbe | World Heritage Gartenreich Dessau-Wörlitz

THOMAS WEISS (Text)
ROLAND KRAWULSKY (Fotografie)
MARGARET WILL (Translation)

HINSTORFF

Sonnenaufgang über Wörlitz, im Hintergrund der Turm von St. Petri
Sunrise over Wörlitz, with the tower of St. Peter's Church in the background

I.

Eigentlich erschließt sich die weiträumige Ausdehnung des Gartenreichs zwischen Dessau und Wörlitz am besten aus der Vogelperspektive. Einen genussvollen Rundblick, wäre er inzwischen nicht zugewachsen, böte eventuell auch der Wildeberg bei Wörlitz, der mit knapp achtzig Metern höchsten natürlichen Erhebung innerhalb der sonst weitgehend flachen Auenlandschaft. Vielleicht deswegen bediente sich der Romancier Jean Paul, der die Residenzstadt des Fürsten Franz von Anhalt-Dessau und dessen berühmten Landschaftsgarten gar dreimal besucht hatte, in seinem 1801 erschienenen *Seebuch des Luftschiffers Giannozzo* einer fiktiven Montgolfiere, um seine erdachten Eindrücke aus der Höhe über der Landschaft wiederzugeben: »Mit der Sonne sank ich da in den wechselnden Garten, dessen Aussichten wieder Gärten sind. Da war mir, als gehe die Sonne eben auf; alle Tempel blitzten wie von Morgenlicht – erfrischender Tau überquoll den Boden, und die Morgenlieder der Lerchen flogen umher.«

Vor allem um sich in seinem an Erhebungen armen Reich besser orientieren zu können, hatte der anhaltische Landesherr in seinem damals siebenhundert Quadratkilometer großen Fürstentum schlankwüchsige, italienischen Zypressen ähnelnde Schwarzpappeln als natürliche Orientierungspunkte sowie hohe, zumeist neugotische Kirchtürme als gebaute Landmarken gesetzt. Der Turm der St.-Petri-Kirche in Wörlitz ist der höchste unter diesen architektonischen Meisterwerken.

Wie fremd und zugleich faszinierend diese Landschaft selbst auf einen so weit Gereisten wie den österreichischen Militär Wilhelm Friedrich von Meyern wirkte, bringt dieser 1804 zum

I.

The great expanse of the *Gartenreich*, or "Garden Kingdom," between Dessau and Wörlitz is really seen best from a bird's eye view. Wildeberg near Wörlitz, at 80 meters the highest natural spot in an otherwise mostly flat floodplain, would also offer a pleasurable panorama, if it hadn't become so overgrown. Perhaps that was why the novelist Jean Paul, who had visited the court seat of Prince Franz of Anhalt-Dessau with its famous landscape garden no less than three times, used a fictitious hot air balloon in his *Seebuch des Luftschiffers Giannozzo*, published in 1801, to convey his imagined impressions from up above the landscape: "I sank with the sun into the changing garden, whose vistas are gardens in turn. To me it was as if the sun was actually coming up; all the temples shone as if from morning light – refreshing dew spilled over the ground and the morning songs of the larks flew about."

Primarily to be able to orient himself better in his own lands, a duchy covering some seven hundred square kilometers at the time but lacking in heights, the Anhalt prince had slender black poplars resembling Italian cypresses planted as natural points of orientation and tall, mostly Neo-Gothic church towers constructed as built landmarks. The tower of St. Peter's Church in Wörlitz is the highest of these architectural masterworks.

How strange and at the same time fascinating this landscape was even to such widely-traveled men as the Austrian military officer Wilhelm Friedrich von Meyern was noted by the latter in 1804, in an account of his sojourn in Dessau four years earlier. He could never really feel at home in flat country, wrote von

Ausdruck, als er von seinem vier Jahre zurückliegenden Dessau-Aufenthalt schreibt: Recht heimisch könne er im Flachland nicht werden »ich kenne nur eine Ebene, die wie ein heiliges Geheimniß immer neu und wechselnd dem Auge sich entschleiert – die des Landes Dessau. Aber dort hat ein trefflicher Mann, mit festem Sinn für alles Schöne, nach diesem innern Gesetze seines Geistes gebildet, der, was er im dreißigsten Jahr freudig begann, im siebzigsten noch eben so freudig fortgesetzt. Jedes Land könnte dem seinen gleichen, wenn das arme Menschengeschlecht nicht meistens eine Heerde wäre, die nur nach Futter blökt. Von jeher zeigt sich da, wo der Trieb zum Schönen der herrschende war, die Menschheit in ihrer reinsten Blüte.«

Im Grunde genommen bietet sich für einen Besuch des Gartenreichs jede Jahreszeit an. Die Mehrzahl der Besucher kommt verständlicherweise in den warmen Sommermonaten. Spezialisten der Gartenkunst jedoch bevorzugen den Herbst oder gar den Winter, wenn die Laubbäume ihre Blätter verloren haben und sich die ganze Qualität ihres Wuchses zeigt. Welche Jahreszeit man auch persönlich bevorzugt, stets empfiehlt es sich, ausreichend Zeit einzuplanen, um möglichst viele der zahlreichen Sehenswürdigkeiten des 142 km² großen Gebietes zu entdecken.

Auf konfektionierte Erlebnisse darf man jedoch hier nicht hoffen und am besten bewegt man sich bei seinen individuellen Erkundigungen mit dem Fahrrad fort oder macht sich zu Fuß auf den Weg: auch als Einspruch gegen das schnelle Lebenstempo als Begleiterscheinung unserer hoch technisierten Welt. Erst so erlebt man die innerhalb der Stadt gelegenen, weltberühmten Bauwerke des neben dem Gartenreich zweiten UNESCO-Welterbes, des Bauhauses sowie den in deren direkter Nachbarschaft

Meyern: "I know only one plain that unveils itself to the eye like a holy secret, forever new and changing – that of the land of Dessau. But there an excellent man with a sure sense for everything beautiful, informed by the inner laws of his intellect, happily continues to do at seventy what he had begun just as happily at thirty. Every land could be like his if the poor human race was not generally a flock that only bleats for food. From time immemorial, mankind shows its purest bloom where the drive for the beautiful has been dominant."

Although any season of the year is appropriate for a visit to the Garden Kingdom, the majority of visitors understandably come in the warm summer months. Specialists in garden design, however, prefer fall or even winter, when the deciduous trees have lost their leaves and the quality of their growth is fully displayed. Whatever season one personally prefers, it is always advisable to plan enough time to discover as many of the numerous sights as possible in an area that covers 142 square kilometers.

No "pre-packaged" experiences should be expected, and individual explorations are best undertaken on a bicycle or on foot, not least as a protest against the fast tempo that is a symptom of our high-tech world. This is the way to experience the world-famous Bauhaus buildings in Dessau – a second UNESCO World Heritage site here, in addition to the Garden Kingdom – as well as the extensive Georgengarten (Georgium) nearby and the other parks on the south side of the Elbe, lined up like pearls threaded on a string. The royal landscape designers were remarkably successful at realizing their main intention, namely the invisibility of the gardens' borders, so that one sometimes quite

Gondel vor dem Monument in Schochs Garten, Wörlitzer Anlagen
Gondola in front of the building known as the Monument in Schoch's Garden, Wörlitz Park

Die Hohe Brücke in den Wörlitzer Anlagen im Herbst …
High Bridge in Wörlitz Park in the fall …

… und im Winter
… and in the winter

Blick zum Vasenhaus in dem von Prinz Johann Georg, dem jüngeren Bruder des Fürsten Franz, geschaffenen Georgium
View toward the House of Vases in Georgium, the landscape garden of Prince Franz's younger brother, Prince Johann Georg

befindlichen weitläufigen Georgengarten und ebenso die anderen südlich der Elbe liegenden Parkanlagen, die sich, wie auf einer Schnur aufgezogen, einer Perlenkette ähnlich, aneinanderreihen. Es ist den fürstlichen Gartengestaltern in bemerkenswerter Weise gelungen, die zentrale Absicht, nämlich die Unsichtbarkeit der Gartengrenzen, umzusetzen, sodass man sich manchmal ganz unvermittelt in einem suggestiven Gartenbild wähnt: etwa einem arkadischen Bereich, wo man hinter jedem Gebüsch Faune erwartet und in jedem Tümpel hingebungsvolle Nymphen.

Abgesehen von der Zeit, die man mitbringen muss, sind es vor allem Neugierde und offene Augen, die unsere Aufmerksamkeit lenken, ja generell Motor unseres Bildungsanspruchs sein sollten. Ungefähr zwanzig Kilometer liegen zwischen der alten Residenzstadt Dessau und der Stadt Wörlitz, dem Höhepunkt der vornehmlich im 18. Jahrhundert gestalteten, ästhetisch und ökologisch wertvollen Kulturlandschaft. In Jahrtausenden gewachsen und im Wesentlichen von den im Jahreslauf wechselnden Wasserständen der zumeist ruhig und gemächlich dahinströmenden Elbe und Mulde geprägt, liegt diese flache Auenlandschaft vor uns wie in einem Geschichtsbuch der Melioration. Das Gebiet ist das Ergebnis einer etwa um 1700, unter Fürst Leopold I., dem »Alten Dessauer« einsetzenden Landreform. Sie hatte zum Ziel, mittels moderner landwirtschaftlicher Methoden die eigene wirtschaftliche Situation zu verbessern, unter anderem durch einen Wechsel von der damals üblichen Dreifelderwirtschaft mit ihrer Brachephase zur Fruchtwechselwirtschaft. Daran war auch die Anlage eines differenzierten Grabensystems gekoppelt, um das Hinterland zu entwässern. Manche der damals ausgehobenen Fließgräben erfüllen ihren Zweck bis heute. An-

suddenly imagines oneself within an evocative picture of a garden: an Arcadian realm, for instance, where fauns could be expected behind every bush and passionate nymphs in every pool.

In addition to having enough time, we should let ourselves be guided by curiosity and open eyes; indeed, these should be the motor driving our need for personal development. Approximately 20 kilometers separate Dessau, the seat of the former court, and Wörlitz, the zenith of this aesthetically and ecologically valuable cultural landscape designed primarily in the 18th century. This flat floodplain, which evolved over thousands of years, is marked by the seasonal changes in the water level of the usually quiet and leisurely flowing Elbe and Mulde rivers.

Now a virtual history book of land improvement, the region reflects a land reform that began around 1700 under Prince Leopold I, known as the "Old Dessauer." The goal of the reform was to improve the local economic situation through utilization of modern agricultural methods, including a shift from the customary three-field system with its fallow phase to crop rotation farming. This was coupled with construction of a sophisticated network of ditches to drain the hinterland. Some of the channels excavated at that time still fulfill their original purpose today. Step by step, with the help of old cadastral field maps, other drainage canals that had been filled in over time are now being dug out again. A ditch stretching several hundred meters from Schönitz Lake to the Grotto of the Nymph Egeria on the east edge of Wörlitz Park, for instance, was recently re-opened. Together with the dikes, which run alongside the Elbe and the Mulde and are visible from afar, these waterways help to protect the agrarian landscape.

Blumengartenhaus im Georgium
Flower Garden House in Georgium

Oranienbaum, Blick zum Chinesischen Teehaus
Oranienbaum, view toward the Chinese Teahouse

Luisium, Bogenbrücke und das für Fürstin Louise von Anhalt-Dessau erbaute Landhaus
Luisium, arched bridge and the "Country House" built for Princess Louise of Anhalt-Dessau

dere, zwischenzeitlich eingeebnete Entwässerungskanäle werden anhand der alten Flurkarten Schritt für Schritt wieder geöffnet, wie zuletzt der einige hundert Meter lange Graben vom Schönitzer See zur Grotte der Nymphe Egeria am östlichen Rand des Wörlitzer Parks.

Gemeinsam mit den weithin sichtbaren Deichen längs der Elbe und Mulde verstärken sie den Schutz der Agrarlandschaft.

II.

Über zweihundert Jahre hinweg blieben große Teile des historischen Gartenreichs als ein für den europäischen Raum einzigartiges Gesamtkunstwerk bis in die Gegenwart erhalten. Geschult durch Gelehrte, wie Johann Joachim Winckelmann, war für den humanistisch gesinnten und aufgeklärten Fürsten von Anhalt-Dessau wie für seinen vier Jahre älteren, ihm lebenslang freundschaftlich verbundenen Wegbegleiter und Architekten, den sächsischen Baron Friedrich Wilhelm von Erdmannsdorff, Schlichtheit der Schlüssel zu wahrer Eleganz. Vor allem ihr Hauptwerk, das Wörlitzer Schloss, Zeitgenossen des Fürsten nannten es einfach das *Landhaus*, kann heute als ein Musterbau für die aufgeklärte Welt des 18. Jahrhunderts gelten. Von vielen Besuchern leider immer noch unterschätzt, ordnen sich das in unmittelbarer Nachbarschaft stehende Küchengebäude, der Marstall, St. Petri und das Graue Haus sowie die Mauer am Zedernberg zu einer großartigen Platzanlage, die zu den bedeutendsten Architekturensembles Europas gezählt werden darf.

Rotes Wachhaus in Wörlitz
The Red Guardhouse in Wörlitz

II.

Large parts of the historic Garden Kingdom have survived for more than 200 years and are preserved today as a *Gesamtkunstwerk* unique in Europe. Simplicity was the key to true elegance for the humanistic-minded, enlightened Prince Franz (1740–1817) of Anhalt-Dessau, who had been influenced by scholars such as Johann Joachim Winckelmann, and for his lifelong friend

Die Geschichte dieser *villa suburbana* beginnt mit dem Abriss des vorherigen barocken Jagdpalais.

Erdmannsdorff, ein in Dresden groß gewordener, vielseitiger Gelehrter, zeigt sich bei all seinen Entwürfen als außerordentlich kreativ und immens produktiv. Sein an klassischen Vorbildern in England und Italien geschulter Stil verzichtet auf jede Effekthascherei, ganz im Vertrauen auf die Einfachheit antiker Baukunst. Der fürstliche Bauherr und sein genial begabter Architekt waren modern nicht im Sinne dessen, was man heute mit diesem Wort bezeichnet, sondern im Sinne des bewussten Menschen, der um das Erbe von Kunst und Denken weiß, der eine klare Sicht auf die Vergangenheit und die Gegenwart hat, der seine Verantwortung für die Zukunft kennt. Damit waren beide ihrer Zeit weit voraus.

In Anhalt-Dessau mit der Residenz Dessau als dem politischen und ökonomischen Machtzentrum unterlag seinerzeit alles dem ausgeprägten Gestaltungsdrang des weit gereisten fürstlichen Auftraggebers. Mit dem Bewusstsein eines Souveräns, dabei keine Kompromisse einzugehen, und einem starken Willen zur Erneuerung reformierte er innerhalb von sechs Jahrzehnten sein von etwa 30 000 Untertanen bewohntes Herrschaftsgebiet, das durch die Folgen des Siebenjährigen Krieges und die europäische Finanzkrise des Jahres 1763 erheblich in Mitleidenschaft gezogen war.

Fürst Franz, der elfjährig zum Vollwaisen wurde und bereits im Alter von achtzehn Jahren die Regierungsgeschäfte von seinem Onkel Dietrich übernommen hatte, entwickelte in Anhalt-Dessau ein Flair von aristokratischer Weltoffenheit. Dieses geistige Klima sprach das aufgeklärte Empfinden des europäischen

Schloss Wörlitz
Wörlitz Palace

»*Frühlingserwachen*« *vor dem Wörlitzer Schloss*
"Spring awakening" in front of Wörlitz Palace

and architect Baron Friedrich Wilhelm von Erdmannsdorff, a Saxon four years older than the prince. In particular their main work, Wörlitz Palace (referred to simply as the *Landhaus*, or Country House, by the prince's contemporaries), is now considered a model building for the enlightened world of the 18th century. The adjacent kitchen buildings, the royal stables, St. Peter's Church, the so-called Gray House and the wall along Zedernberg form a superb complex, which numbers among Europe's most

St. Petri mit dem Grauen Haus (links), dem Marstall und dem Küchengebäude
St. Peter's Church with the Gray House (left), the stables and the kitchen building

important architectural ensembles but unfortunately is still often underrated by visitors. The history of this *villa suburbana* began with the demolition of an earlier Baroque hunting lodge.

Erdmannsdorff, a multifaceted scholar who grew up in Dresden, was exceptionally creative and immensely productive, as his designs show. Influenced by classical models in England and Italy, his style dispenses with showiness, trusting completely in the simplicity of classical architecture. The royal client and his brilliantly talented architect were modern not in today's sense of the word, but rather as self-aware men cognizant of the legacy of art and thought, with a clear view of the past and the present coupled with recognition of their responsibility for the future. In this sense both were far ahead of their times.

Publikums so sehr an, dass vor allem Wörlitz bis weit in das 19. Jahrhundert als Allegorie eines idealen Ortes verstanden wurde. »Wörlitz ist das Paradies gewesen« beschreibt 1926 der Kunsthistoriker Wilhelm van Kempen enthusiastisch dieses Phänomen, »danach sich die Menschheit um 1800 sehnte, Wörlitz ist das Mekka gewesen, wohin man gläubigen Herzens pilgerte, in Wörlitz betreten wir heiligen Boden edler Kultur. …, hier wandeln wir in den Spuren Carl Augusts und Goethes, hier lebt Jean Jacques Rousseaus Geist, hier war das Ziel der Reise Winckelmanns.« Der in Stendal geborene Präfekt der römischen Altertümer am Vatikan und homosexuelle Feingeist Winckelmann, der das berühmte Schlagwort »von edler Einfalt und stiller Größe« prägte, hat das Gartenreich leider nie erreicht.

Das, was wir heute – zwischen Dessau und Wörlitz gelegen –, gerne als einen Hort der Aufklärung bezeichnen, ist trotz zahlreicher Veränderungen immer noch allgegenwärtig. Insbesondere mit dem englischen Landschaftsgarten, den Fürst Franz nach Deutschland brachte, ging die politische Bedeutung einher, die diesen Garten zu einer Leitidee der Aufklärung machte. Unsere immerwährende Leidenschaft auf der Suche nach dem Garten Eden scheint hier an Elbe und Mulde eine greifbare Entsprechung gefunden zu haben.

Mit den Wörlitzer Anlagen hat ein vermeintlich unerreichbarer Sehnsuchtstraum Gestalt angenommen. Das war es auch, was die UNESCO im Jahr 2000 veranlasste, das Gartenreich von Dessau-Wörlitz auf die begehrte Liste des Welterbes zu setzen. In der Begründung heißt es, es sei »ein herausragendes Beispiel für die Umsetzung philosophischer Prinzipien der Aufklärung in einer Landschaftsgestaltung, die Kunst, Erziehung und Wirt-

At that time everything in Anhalt-Dessau – where Dessau was the center of political and economic power – was subject to the pronounced creative drive of the widely-traveled prince. Conscious that, as sovereign over a land of 30,000 subjects, he had no need to make compromises, Prince Franz exercised his strong will for renewal over the course of six decades, reforming dominions that had been badly damaged during the Seven Years' War and by the European financial crisis of 1763.

Orphaned at the age of eleven, Prince Franz (who ruled as Leopold III Friedrich Franz) took over government affairs from his uncle Dietrich already at the age of eighteen and proceeded to develop an aristocratic cosmopolitan flair in Anhalt-Dessau. This intellectual climate appealed so much to the enlightened sensibilities of the European public that Wörlitz in particular was regarded as the allegory of an ideal place far into the 19th century. Writing enthusiastically about this phenomenon in 1926, art historian Wilhelm van Kempen remarked, "Wörlitz was the Paradise that mankind was yearning for around 1800, Wörlitz was the Mecca for faithful-hearted pilgrims, in Wörlitz we tread on the holy ground of noble culture. … here we walk in the tracks of Carl August and Goethe, here Jean Jacques Rousseau's spirit lives, here was the goal of Winckelmann's journey." Born in Stendal and later the prefect of Roman antiquities at the Vatican, the homosexual connoisseur Winckelmann – who coined the famous phrase "from noble simplicity and serene grandeur" – unfortunately never reached the Garden Kingdom.

What we like to refer to now as a refuge of the Enlightenment – situated between Dessau and Wörlitz – still exists today, despite numerous changes. In particular, the English landscape

Wörlitz, Pantheon
Wörlitz, Pantheon

Oranienbaum, Doppelbrücke im Englisch-chinesischen Garten
Oranienbaum, double bridge in the English-Chinese Garden

garden, brought to Germany by Prince Franz, went hand in hand with the political significance that made this garden a leitmotif for the Enlightenment. The eternal passion of our search for the Garden of Eden seems to have found a tangible analogy here on the Elbe and Mulde.

A longed-for, supposedly unattainable dream took on form with the Wörlitz gardens. This was also what prompted UNESCO to put the Garden Kingdom of Dessau-Wörlitz on the coveted list of World Heritage sites in 2000. The justification for the inscription calls the site "an outstanding example of the application of the philosophical principles of the Age of Enlightenment

schaft harmonisch miteinander verbindet«. In der Tat sind Bildung, Freiheit und das Recht auf individuelles Glück Grundwerte der hier bis heute wirksam werdenden Ideenwelt. Sie spiegelt sich wider in Architektur und Gartenkunst, die inspiriert von englischen und italienischen Vorbildern ein klassizistisches Gesamtkunstwerk bildet.

III.

Seitdem das Gartenreich in der zweiten Hälfte des 18. Jahrhunderts erschaffen wurde, übt diese Gemütslandschaft ersten Ranges mit ihren atemberaubenden jahreszeitlichen Stimmungsbildern eine magische Anziehungskraft auf Reisende jeder Couleur aus. Hier kann man, wie schon erwähnt, mit dem Rad oder am besten zu Fuß das Glück der Naturerfahrung erleben und spüren, dass die Erde für uns Menschen da ist. Und hier kann man an den Bauwerken sehr gut beobachten, wie Patina entsteht: leise, heimlich und mit Würde – vielleicht ein wenig zu unspektakulär für den modernen Geschmack.

Wer die Flüchtigkeit, mit der viele Menschen heute ihre Umwelt wahrnehmen, überwindet, vermag zu entdecken, dass alles

Seite 26
Schwarzer Sitz im Landschaftsgarten Georgium

Seite 27
Ruine des Schwedenhauses am Weg von Vockerode zum Luisium

to the design of a landscape that integrates art, education and economy in a harmonious whole." Education, freedom and the right to individual happiness are in fact core values in a world of ideas that is still valid here today. These ideas are reflected in architecture and landscape, forming a classicist *Gesamtkunstwerk* inspired by English and Italian models.

III.

Ever since the Garden Kingdom was created in the second half of the 18th century, this inestimable, emotion-evoking landscape with its stunning seasonal ambience has had a magical appeal to travelers of all kinds. Here it is possible – by bicycle or even better on foot, as has already been said – to find happiness in the experience of nature and to sense that the earth is here for us, for mankind. Here one can also observe very well how patina develops: quietly, discreetly, with dignity – perhaps a bit too unspectacular for modern taste.

Anyone who transcends the superficiality with which many people perceive their surroundings today discovers that everything in this earthly Arcadia is filled with yearning and beauty.

page 26
The so-called Black Seat in the Georgium landscape garden

page 27   Ruins of the Swedish House on the way from Vockerode to Luisium

»Schlangenhaus« im Luisium
"Snake House" in Luisium Park

in diesem irdischen Arkadien erfüllt ist von Verlangen und Schönheit. Je nach Sonnenstand, Bewölkung, Regen, Nebel, Schnee wandeln sich die Gartenbilder und soweit man sehen kann, herrscht allerorten Angemessenheit. Nirgendwo vulgäre Opulenz; kein Stein zu wenig, kein Schnörkel zu viel. Gerade weil das Gartenreich kein sentimentales Stimmungsmuseum ist, sondern Gegenstand lebendiger Auseinandersetzung, öffnet sich ein Augenblick der Beobachtung zu dauernder Erkenntnis.

Alle im Gartenreich zwischen Dessau und Wörlitz vom Fürsten Franz und seinen beiden Brüdern, den Prinzen Johann Georg (Georgengarten / Georgium) und Albert (Kühnauer Park) angelegten Landschaftsgärten sind mit Bedacht konzipierte Raumkunstwerke und werden erst durch das sich in ihnen Bewegen angemessen wahrgenommen. Nur auf diese Weise läuft die vom anhaltischen Landesherrn und seinen Hofgärtnern Johann Friedrich Eyserbeck, Johann Christian Neumark oder Johann Leopold Schoch geplante, programmatische Raumfolge Bild für Bild vor den Augen des Spaziergängers ab.

Die in die Natur eingebetteten Blickachsen, die Jean Paul als »glänzende Rennbahnen der Jugend« feierte, sind weit über die Gärten hinaus angelegt und führen das Auge tief in die Auenlandschaft. Diese ist offen, aber auch ihrerseits gegliedert, kennt das Gehölz und den geschwungenen Weg, den Hügel und die Biegung. Sie setzt den gestauten Blick voraus, sie hält die Balance zwischen Natur und Zivilisation, sie gehorcht in jeder Hinsicht dem mittleren Maß. Vom Philosophen Joachim Ritter stammt der Satz: »Landschaft ist Natur, die im Anblick für einen fühlenden und empfindenden Betrachter ästhetisch gegenwärtig ist.«

The gardens' appearance changes according to the position of the sun, to the presence of clouds, rain, fog, or snow; as far as one can see a sense of appropriateness prevails. Nowhere is there vulgar opulence; there is never a stone too few, or an overdone embellishment. Precisely because the Garden Kingdom is not a sentimental "mood museum," but rather an object with which the visitor must actively deal, one moment of observation can bring about lasting awareness.

All the landscape gardens laid out in the Garden Kingdom between Dessau and Wörlitz by Prince Franz and his two brothers, the princes Johann Georg (Georgengarten) and Albert (Kühnauer Park) are carefully conceived spatial works of art. In order to experience them properly, it is necessary to move about within the gardens. Only then do the programmatic spatial sequences planned by the Anhalt princes and their court gardeners Johann Friedrich Eyserbeck, Johann Christian Neumark and Johann Leopold Schoch run their course, scene for scene, before the eyes of the stroller. The axial views, embedded in nature and celebrated by Jean Paul as "youth's bright race courses," are laid out to extend far beyond the gardens, leading the eye deep into the floodplain. This is an open landscape, but it, too, has its ordering elements: groves, winding paths, hills, curves. It presupposes blocked views, keeps a balance between nature and civilization, and in every respect obeys the happy medium. As the philosopher Joachim Ritter has said, "Landscape is nature which the observer, in viewing it, senses and regards as aesthetically present."

The landscape gardens are thus tied to the experience of strolling about in them. The rhythms and dynamics inherent in garden

Blick zum Venustempel in Schochs Garten (Wörlitz)
View toward the Venus Temple in Schoch's Garden (Wörlitz)

Die Landschaftsgärten sind also an die Erfahrung ihrer Begehbarkeit gebunden. Die in den Gartenbildern innewohnende Rhythmik und Dynamik überträgt sich in den feinsten Nuancen auf den Spaziergänger und es erschließen sich die auf das Sensibelste ausbalancierten Kompositionen. Mit ihrer unverblümten Gegenwärtigkeit stellen sie einen idealen Erfahrungsgrund für den vom Lärm geplagten Menschen dar.

Eine Hirn- und Herzensangelegenheit war das Spazierengehen auch dem berühmten französischen Naturphilosophen Rousseau. Ihm setzte Fürst Franz in aufrichtiger Bewunderung ein Denkmal: eine mit Pappeln bestandene Insel in den Wörlitzer Anlagen, die frappierend derjenigen im Park von Ermenonville bei Senlis im Norden von Paris gleicht. Für den im Zentrum der kleinen Insel befindlichen, von einer Urne bekrönten Gedenkstein verfasste der Fürst selbst die Inschrift:

»Dem Andenken J. J. Rousseau / Bürgers zu Genf / der die Witzlinge zum gesunden Verstand / die Wollüstigen zum wahren Genuss / die irrende Kunst zur Einfalt der Natur / die Zweifler zum Trost der Offenbarung / mit männlicher Beredsamkeit zurückwies. / Er starb den 2. Juli 1778.«

Die in Johann Wolfgang von Goethes *Wahlverwandtschaften* enthaltenen, von peniblen Philologen auf mehr als zwei Dutzend bezifferten Spaziergänge zeigen die hohe Wichtigkeit der Zu-Fuß-Erkundung von Landschaftsgärten auch für den berühmten Dichter an. Goethe ließ sich zu dem 1809 erschienenen Roman von insgesamt acht Wörlitz-Besuchen inspirieren, wobei er sich bei seinen Wandelgängen ganz dem Garten überließ. »Nach nichts zu suchen, das war mein Sinn«, notierte der Frankfurter in Weimar.

scenes are communicated in their finest nuances to the stroller, and sensitively balanced compositions are revealed. With their straightforward presence they offer noise-plagued man an ideal place for introspection and observation.

For the French philosopher Rousseau, walking was a matter of both heart and mind. Prince Franz erected a monument to Rousseau in the Wörlitz gardens, as a sign of his sincere admiration: an island planted with poplars, astoundingly similar to the one in the park at Ermenonville near Senlis in the north of Paris. The prince himself wrote the inscription for the memorial stone, placed in the center of the island and crowned with an urn:

"In memory of J. J. Rousseau / citizen of Geneva / who with manly eloquence turned / the joke-makers back to good sense / the salacious back to true pleasure / erring art back to the simplicity of nature / the skeptic back to the solace of the revelation. / He died on 2 July 1778."

The walks mentioned in Johann Wolfgang von Goethe's *Wahlverwandtschaften (Elective Affinities)* – according to fastidious philologists, they number over two dozen – demonstrate the great importance that the famous writer put on the exploration of landscape gardens on foot. A total of eight visits to Wörlitz inspired Goethe for this novel, published in 1809. On his strolls he gave himself over completely to the garden: "… seeking nothing, that was my intention," wrote the Frankfurt native in Weimar.

Today many of us can only partly decipher the meaning of the references to be found throughout the gardens, and they sometimes even strike us as a bit strange – perhaps we have lost our sensibility. Nonetheless the garden scenes offer large numbers

Gotisches Haus in den Wörlitzer Anlagen, Gartenseite
Gothic House in Wörlitz Park, garden side

Wörlitz, Rousseau-Insel im Morgenlicht
Wörlitz, Rousseau Island in morning light

Wenn auch die inhaltlichen Bezüge für viele heute nur noch bedingt zu entschlüsseln sind und manchmal sogar ein wenig befremdlich wirken, – womöglich ist uns die Empfindsamkeit abhanden gekommen –, so bieten doch die Gartenbilder den zahlreichen, spazierenden Besuchern einen harmonischen Augentrost in einem Zeitalter optischer und akustischer Umweltverschmutzung. Auf der Suche nach dem erfüllten Augenblick

mischen sich mittlerweile allerdings auch hier die Töne der Zivilisation in den zarten Schmelz des Wohlklangs, der über allem liegt.

In jüngster Zeit sind es hauptsächlich die Errungenschaften moderner Umwelttechnologie, beispielsweise die Windräder bei Zieko, die nicht einmal vor dem Gartenreich Halt machen.

Diese Schrunden kann der vergängliche Mantel überirdischer Schönheit nicht überdecken und auch die, von dem in der antiken Mythologie bewanderten Fürsten überall im Gartenreich platzierten Gottheiten können da nicht helfen. Als Skulpturen in Nischen flankieren sie Hausportale oder stehen einsam und erhaben auf Podesten inmitten der Gartenlandschaft. Vor allem Venus, die in ihrer unbekleideten, makellosen Schönheit unschwer erkennbare Göttin, ist mehrmals präsent. Ein Gleiches gilt für den sterblichen Ganymed, der »als der Schönste geboren war« (Homer) und als Mundschenk des Zeus überraschend häufig in den Häusern des Gartenreichs symbolisch seinen Dienst verrichtet, sodass der eine oder andere homoerotische Anspielungen vermuten könnte.

Andere Figuren bedürfen einer gesteigerten Aufmerksamkeit, da sie sich nur dem kenntnisreichen Spaziergänger mitteilen. Beispielsweise Priapos, der Sohn des Dionysos und der Aphrodite: Von erotischer Lust inspiriert, verrät er durch nichts weiter als eine Beetbepflanzung in Form eines monströsen Phallus am Fuße des Wörlitzer Flora-Tempels seine Anwesenheit. Der aus Gründen der Schicklichkeit kaum wahrnehmbare Gott der Gärten und der unerschöpflichen Potenz sorgte leidenschaftlich für die Amouren des Landesherrn mit Luise Schoch im Gotischen Haus, in deren Folge die Tochter des Fürstlich-Anhaltischen Hofgärtners zur Mutter dreier gemeinsamer Kinder wurde.

of strolling visitors harmonious solace for the eye in an era of visual and acoustic pollution. But as we search for moments of fulfillment we find that here, too, the sounds of civilization are now mingling with the subtle, mellifluous harmony which lies over everything.

Lately it has primarily been feats of modern environmental technology, such as the windmills near Zieko, that do not make concessions even for the Garden Kingdom.

The ephemeral cloak of transcendental beauty cannot conceal these cracks, and not even the gods, placed all over the Garden Kingdom by a prince well-versed in classical mythology, are able to help. They flank portals, as sculptures in niches, or stand alone and sublime on pedestals in the midst of the gardens. Venus in particular, a goddess easily recognized by her unclothed, flawless beauty, is depicted several times. The same is true of Ganymede, born "as the handsomest man among all mortal men" (Homer). As Zeus's cupbearer he is found doing symbolic service surprisingly often in the buildings of the Garden Kingdom, suggesting one or another homoerotic allusion. Other figures require more concentration because they disclose their identity only to the knowledgeable. For instance Priapus, the son of Dionysus and Aphrodite: inspired by erotic lust, he betrays his presence through nothing more than the planting of a bed in the form of a monstrous phallus at the foot of the Flora Temple in Wörlitz. This god of gardens and inexhaustible virility, barely discernible for reasons of propriety, was a passionate support of the amours between the prince and Luise Schoch, daughter of the Anhalt court gardener, in the Gothic House, as a result of which she bore him three children.

Jagdgöttin Diana (links) und Faun, Sieglitzer Berg
Diana, goddess of the hunt (left), and a faun, Sieglitz Hill

Vestalin-Figur im Tempel der Nacht, Insel Stein (Wörlitz)
Vestal virgin in the Temple of the Night, Stone Island (Wörlitz)

Das Rittertor im Landschaftspark Großkühnau am Abend
Knight's Gate in Grosskühnau Park in the evening

Wenn sich gegen Abend das Elysium der heidnischen Antike leert, das Wassergeflügel seine Aufgeregtheiten abgelegt hat und Ruhe einkehrt, merkt man, wie kostbar Stille ist. Haben noch vor wenigen Stunden Hunderte Flaneure das Herzstück des Gartenreichs, die Wörlitzer Anlagen genossen, hört man nun kein Geräusch mehr um die Gebäude, Gedenksteine und Statuen. Friedrich von Matthissons Empfindungen für solche besonderen Stimmungen im Gartenreich veranlasste ihn zu diesen lyrischen Zeilen: »Stille! Du verklärst der trüben / Zukunft Nebelgraun; / Lehrst uns glauben, hoffen, lieben, / und belohnst mit Selbstvertraun!«

Toward evening, when the Elysium of heathen antiquity becomes empty of visitors, when the water birds have stopped their flutter and all is quiet, one notices how precious tranquility is. Although only a few hours earlier hundreds of strollers had been enjoying the Wörlitz gardens, the heart of the Garden Kingdom, not a sound is to be heard now around the buildings, monuments and statues. Friedrich von Matthisson's perception of the special moods of the Garden Kingdom prompted him to pen these lyrics: "Tranquility! You transfigure the gray fog of the dim future; / teach us faith, hope and love, / and reward us with self-confidence!"

IV.

Vom Flugplatz in Dessau aus, der in den 30iger Jahren des 20. Jahrhunderts insbesondere durch die Flugzeuglegende *Tante Ju* von Hugo Junkers Weltberühmtheit erlangte, könnte man theoretisch, wie Jean Pauls erfundener *Luftschiffer Giannozzo,* mit einem Fesselballon höchst komfortabel das gesamte Gartenreich erkunden. Solcherlei Luftfahrten, wie sie auch der 1909 durch die Dessauer Continental-Gasgesellschaft gegründete Anhaltische Verein für Luftschifffahrt wiederbeleben wollte, sind jedoch selten. Die meisten Besucher gelangen über die Autobahn, von Süden aus über Leipzig oder von Norden aus Berlin kommend, in die schwach besiedelte Region. Der auf diesem Weg Kommende wird als Erstes der mächtige Architekturkomplex des Braunkohlekraftwerks in Vockerode gewahr. Über viele Jahrzehnte war

IV.

From the Dessau airport, which gained world renown in the 1930s primarily through Hugo Junkers's legendary airplane *Tante Ju*, it would theoretically be possible to study the entire Garden Kingdom quite comfortably from a tethered balloon, like Jean Paul's fictitious *Luftschiffer Giannozzo*. But such aerial voyages are rare, even though the Anhaltischer Verein für Luftschifffahrt (Anhalt Airship Association), founded in 1909 by the Dessauer Continental-Gasgesellschaft, wanted to revive them. Most visitors arrive in this sparsely settled region on the autobahn, coming from the south via Leipzig or from the north via Berlin, and the first thing they catch sight of is the mighty architectural complex of the brown coal power plant in Vockerode. The former fishing village was dependent for decades on the power

Wörlitz, Abendstimmung am Nymphaeum
Wörlitz, evening at the Nymphaeum

Abendstimmung nahe der Elbe
Evening light near the Elbe

das einstige Fischerdorf vom Kraftwerk abhängig. Es gab den Menschen wirtschaftliche Sicherheit, zugleich lagerten sich jedoch hunderte Tonnen Flugasche in der Umgebung ab. Als das Werk 1994 vom Netz genommen wurde, hinterließ es Arbeitslosigkeit und eine riesige Industriebrache. Nach einem Teilabriss im September 2001 hat der Bau seinen Denkmalstatus eingebüßt. Zusammen mit dem daneben stehenden Gasturbinenwerk und der ebenfalls brachliegenden Fläche ehemaliger Gewächshausanlagen erinnert es dennoch unübersehbar an den einst blühenden Industriestandort.

In Anbetracht dessen ist es kaum vorstellbar, welche landschaftlichen und kulturellen Reize im Hinterland versteckt liegen.

Doch ungeachtet aus welcher Richtung man sich dem Gartenreich nähert, dem Aufmerksamen fällt sofort die üppige Vegetation beidseits der Straßen ins Auge. Auf der Landstraße von Dessau-Waldersee in östlicher Richtung, gegen Wörlitz zu, gleicht die Reise auf den gekurvten, manchmal engen Straßen nahezu einer Fahrt durch einen grünen Tunnel mit naturbelassenem Wildwuchs.

Gelegentlich bietet die Landschaft aber auch Ausblicke, bei denen sich von Kopfweiden gesäumte Bachläufe und mit Schilf bestandene Altwasserflächen der Elbe mit offenen Acker- oder Wiesenflächen abwechslungsreich zu einem unvergesslichen Bild ergänzen.

Bereits seit dem 18. Jahrhundert definieren in diesem Bereich in Reih und Glied gepflanzte Obstbäume, pittoresk platzierte Baumgruppen und knorrige Solitäreichen den Raum und bieten dem Betrachter angenehme Haltepunkte. Dazwischen bilden

station, which provided economic security but at the same time deposited hundreds of tons of flue ash in the surroundings. When the complex was removed from the power network in 1994, unemployment and a huge industrial wasteland were left in its wake. Partial demolition in September 2001 cost the complex its status as a historic monument. The brown coal works, an adjacent gas turbine plant and a now unused complex of greenhouses are an obvious reminder that industry once flourished here. It is hard to imagine that scenic and cultural attractions could exist in the countryside beyond them.

But no matter from which direction one approaches the Garden Kingdom, the alert observer immediately notices the luxurious vegetation on both sides of the road. On the route from Dessau-Waldersee to the east, going toward Wörlitz, the trip along the curving, sometimes narrow road is almost like driving through a green tunnel of rank growth. Sometimes, however, the landscape opens up to an unforgettable scene, with views of creeks lined with pollard willows or of reed-filled backwaters from the Elbe, alternating with open cropland or meadows.

Ever since the 18th century this region has been defined by rows of fruit trees, picturesquely sited groups of trees, and gnarled solitary oaks which offer the observer pleasant places to tarry. In between are the remnants of once-numerous avenues of trees, a network that offers unsuspected potential for traveling about the territory. Since 1985 the oaks that had increasingly disappeared from the landscape are being replanted on the floodplain; today there are again around 20,000 oaks in the river meadows. In the Garden Kingdom these mighty trees, marking the transition from the open floodplains to the dense alluvial forests,

Reste einstmals zahlreicher Alleen ein territoriales System, das immer noch ein ungeahntes Mobilitätsangebot bereithält. Seit 1985 werden die zuvor mehr und mehr aus dem Landschaftsbild verschwunden Eichen auf den Auenwiesen nachgepflanzt, sodass es heute wieder um zwanzigtausend Wieseneichen gibt. Im Gartenreich kennzeichnen die mächtigen Bäume den Übergang der offenen Auenflächen zum dichten Auwald und bieten wertvolle Lebensräume für selten geworden Tierarten wie den Hirschkäfer oder den vom Aussterben bedrohten Heldbock, der auch als Großer Eichenbock bezeichnet wird. Die Brutbäume dieser Käferart müssen einen Stammumfang von mindestens einem Meter haben und sollen nach Süden frei stehen, damit sie die Mittagssonne besser einfangen.

Manche begeisterte Naturfreunde meinen nicht zu Unrecht, dass man, um das Gartenreich verstehen zu können, den Lebensrhythmus der Bäume annehmen müsse. Ganz so, wie der von Fürst Franz geschätzte römische Großdichter Vergil es in seiner *Georgica – Über den Landbau* formulierte: »Jegliches Obst das fruchtbar im Blütengewande des Lenzes barg der Baum / Er trug es gereift dem Herbst entgegen.« Vor allem im Frühjahr, wenn die Bäume der Streuobstwiesen oder aber diejenigen entlang der oft kilometerlangen Alleen in voller Blüte stehen, wird einem deutlich, dass sich Fürst Franz auch als oberster Gärtner seines Landes verstand und wie er, als Teil seines von Horaz entlehnten ästhetischen Credos, stets das Nützliche mit dem Angenehmen in idealer Weise zu verbinden wusste.

In der Ferne, oder aber manchmal auch ganz nah, entdeckt man auf Erkundungsfahrten und -gängen zahlreiche, wie zufällig hineinkomponierte Bauwerke und Gedenksteine und spürt

offer valuable habitats for rare animal species such as the stag beetle or the endangered Great Capricorn beetle. The nesting trees of the latter have to have a circumference of at least one meter and need to be exposed toward the south to better capture the midday sun.

Some zealous nature lovers believe, not without good reason, that one must understand the natural rhythm of the trees in order to appreciate the Garden Kingdom, an idea formulated by Prince Franz's cherished Roman poet Virgil in his *Georgics – On Working the Earth:* "And all the fruits wherewith in early bloom / The orchard tree had clothed her, in full tale / hung there, by mellowing autumn perfected." Particularly in the springtime when the trees are in full bloom in the orchard meadows or along the avenues, which often stretch for kilometers, it becomes clear that Prince Franz also considered himself his realm's chief gardener. As part of the aesthetic credo he borrowed from Horace, he moreover always understood how to combine usefulness with pleasure in an ideal manner.

On exploratory drives or walks, one discovers in the distance – or sometimes even quite close – numerous structures and monuments that appear to be placed in the gardens as if by chance, and one increasingly senses the Arcadian beauty of the landscape scenes. Various historic styles give the buildings their distinctive appearance. An inn resembling a medieval castle or a simple guardhouse on the embankment, constructed of bog ore rocks in the form of a hermitage: each once served as a place to linger. Here, where landscape and architecture seem to have joined with one another in an ideal manner, hardly anything disturbs the perfect symbiosis. In Goethe's words: "Nature and Art, they

Solitäreiche in der Elbaue bei Großkühnau
Solitary oak in the Elbe river meadows near Grosskühnau

mehr und mehr die arkadische Schönheit der Landschaftsbilder. Verschiedene historische Stile geben den Gebäuden ihr unverwechselbares Gesicht. Ob als einer mittelalterlichen Burg ähnliches Gasthaus oder einfaches, von Raseneisenstein bewehrtes Wallwachhaus in Form einer Eremitage, dienten sie einst als Ort der Einkehr. Hier, wo sich Landschaft und Architektur in idealer Weise miteinander verbündet zu haben scheinen, stört kaum etwas die perfekte Symbiose. Mit den Worten Goethes: »Natur und Kunst, sie scheinen sich zu fliehen / und haben sich, eh man es denkt, gefunden.« In Anlehnung an die berühmten Vorbilder in England komplettierten weiße Kühe oder weißes Damwild das pastorale Gartenbild und die einst in der Nähe des Wörlitzer Schlosses gehaltenen Pfauen (heute am Gotischen Haus) symbolisierten die unstillbare Sehnsucht nach Glück.

Während das Schloss von Großkühnau, die klassizistischen Landhäuser im Georgengarten, Luisium und in Wörlitz sowie die barocken Palais von Oranienbaum und Mosigkau auf den ersten Blick annähernd unbeschadet die Zeit überstanden haben, hinterließen zwei Jahrhunderte auch Ruinen, welche die einstige Schönheit kaum mehr erkennen lassen. Einige wichtige Bauwerke wie die Solitude, ein antikisierender Tempel, sind bis auf das Fundament und ein paar Sandsteinfragmente vollkommen verschwunden. Allerdings keimt auch Hoffnung auf. Einsam lagen die Ruinenreste noch bis vor kurzem zwischen den hoch aufragenden Bäumen im *Waldpark der Einsamkeit*. Während das Küchengebäude in unmittelbarer Nachbarschaft wohl noch länger seiner Auferstehung entgegensehen muss, scheint der Wiederaufbau der Solitude inzwischen gesichert. Das Wasser der Elbe hat sich seit dem 18. Jahrhundert in einiger Entfernung ein neues

go their separate way, / It seems; yet all at once they find each other."

Following the famous prototypes in England, white cows or white fallow deer complemented the pastoral garden scene, and peacocks, once kept close to Wörlitz Palace (and now found at the Gothic House), symbolized man's unquenchable yearning for happiness.

The palace at Grosskühnau, the classicist "country houses" in Georgengarten, Luisium and Wörlitz and the Baroque palaces of Oranienbaum and Mosigkau seem at first glance to have survived irrespective of time, but two centuries have also left behind ruins whose former beauty is hard to perceive today. Several important structures, including the Solitude, a classical temple, have completely disappeared except for their foundations and a few sandstone fragments. But hope is burgeoning. Until a short time ago the ruins lay forlorn among the towering trees in the so-called Forest Park of Solitude. Whereas the nearby kitchen building will probably have to wait longer for its resurrection, reconstruction of the Solitude now appears assured. The waters of the Elbe have found a new bed some distance away since the 18th century, and they only return when spring and fall flooding fills the broad sinks in the meadowlands, as if to check on the Solitude's progress.

Similar to how the melt waters from the glacier thrust reshaped this landscape 150,000 years ago, the waters of the Elbe flood this area in a regular seasonal rhythm. The natural river meadow, the only one of this size still extant in Germany, with the largest contiguous alluvial forest in central Europe, is an established ecological system which does not tolerate speed or abrupt changes.

Landschaftspark Großkühnau, Weinbergschlösschen
Grosskühnau Park, vineyard "palace"

Landhaus (Schloss) Georgium
"Country House" (palace) in Georgium

»Alte Stuterei« im Landschaftspark Luisium
"Old Stud Farm" in Luisium Park

Bett geschaffen und nur wenn die Überflutungen des Frühjahrs und des Herbstes die weiten Senken der Aue füllen, kehrt sie zurück, gleichsam um nachzusehen, welche Fortschritte das Bauwerk nimmt.

Ähnlich wie die Schmelzwässer des Gletscher-Vorstoßes vor 150 000 Jahren diese Landschaft überformten, überschwemmt das Wasser der Elbe in jahreszeitlichem Rhythmus regelmäßig die Flächen. Diese naturnahe Stromaue, die einzige, die wir in solchen Ausmaßen in Deutschland noch besitzen, mit dem größten zusammenhängenden Auenwaldkomplex Mitteleuropas ist ein gewachsenes Ökosystem, das Geschwindigkeit und abrupte Veränderungen nicht verträgt. Noch vor etwa eintausend Jahren konnte sich bei Hochwasser der gemächlich dahinfließende Strom beiderseits bis zu zehn Kilometer in das Hinterland ausbreiten. Die Deiche, die etwa seit dem 17. Jahrhundert das Flussbett der Elbe auf beiden Ufern begleiten, bieten den Menschen bei Hochwasser – wie die Jahrhundertflut im Jahr 2002 gezeigt hat – nur bedingt Schutz vor den Wassermassen. In weiser Voraussicht, ganz in Kenntnis der Gefahren, hatte Fürst Franz schon 1795 am nordwestlichen Ende des Schönitzer Sees die sogenannten Neun Hügel als Deichschutz gegen das Treibeis errichten lassen. Daran erinnert bis heute ein klassizistisch gestalteter Gedenkstein (Proteus-Stein): »Höret Nachkommen / eine euch warnende / Stimme / vorsichtiger Fleiss schuf / diese Hügel und dieses Gebüsch / um die feldbewahrenden Dämme / vor dem zerstörenden Eise / zu schützen / wendet alles an / sie zu erhalten.«

Ständige Pflege, unter anderem auch eine intensivere Beweidung mit Schafen, sollen heutzutage die Dämme kontinuierlich stabilisieren. In jüngster Zeit gesteht man der Elbe zusätzlich

Ruine der Solitude am Sieglitzer Berg
Ruins of the temple "Solitude" on Sieglitz Hill

Rauhes Wachhaus am Fliederwall nahe Vockerode
Guardhouse built of coarse bog ore, on the lilac embankment near Vockerode

Kanalseite des Gotischen Hauses in den Wörlitzer Anlagen
Canal side of the Gothic House in Wörlitz Park

Only a thousand years ago the floodwaters of the leisurely flowing river could still spread out into the hinterland as far as ten kilometers on either side. The dikes, which have paralleled the riverbed of the Elbe on both banks since around the 17th century, offer man only limited protection from high water – as the major flood in 2002 demonstrated. Quite aware of the dangers, Prince Franz wisely had the so-called Nine Hills erected in 1795 at the northwest end of Schönitz Lake, as a protective dike against drifting ice. A classically designed monument, the Proteus Stone, is a reminder today of this undertaking: "Listen descendants / to a warning / voice / cautious diligence created / these hills

Polderflächen zu, in die sich der Fluss bei Hochwasser gezielt ausbreiten kann.

Der *furor hortensis* – so wurde in England der Sieg der Landschaftsgärten über die barocken Vorgängeranlagen bezeichnet – den Fürst Franz während mehrerer Reisen nach England erlebte, jener Zorn hatte den jungen Landesherren bereits in frühen Jahren ereilt. Nicht nur für die englischen Aristokraten, die der Fürst auf ihren weitläufigen Landgütern besuchte, sondern auch für ihn gehörten alsbald »ein großer Raum, ein geschlängelter Fluss und ein Wald« zu den absoluten Notwendigkeiten des Lebens, ohne die ein Gentleman mit seinem Land keine gute Figur machen konnte.

Wie stark sich der anhaltische Landesherr insgesamt einen anglophilen Lebensstil zu eigen machte, demonstrierte er unter anderem durch seinen »englischen« roten Rock, mit dem er sich von dem seinerzeit hochgeschätzten Maler Anton von Maron in einem großfigurigen Porträt in Szene setzen ließ. Vermutlich wollte er dabei dem Betrachter signalisieren, dass dieses Kostüm für ihn nicht nur eine elegante Hülle war, sondern eine charakterbildende Wirkung hatte, sozusagen eine bestimmte Art sich zu geben nahelegte.

So blickt Fürst Franz bis heute im Speisesaal des Wörlitzer Landhauses im Kreise seiner ebenfalls auf Leinwand gebannten Vorfahren auf sein Lebenswerk herab: eben nicht mit standesgemäßer Herablassung, sondern er scheint eher auf eine unbestimmte Weise beseelt und man spürt, dass sich seine Versunkenheit gleichermaßen auf Vergangenes wie auf Künftiges richten könnte.

Wörlitz, Synagoge (vorne) und St.-Petri-Kirche
Wörlitz, synagogue (foreground) and St. Peter's Church

and these bushes / to safeguard the dams that protect the fields from the destructive ice / do everything to preserve them."

Sustained care, including intensive grazing by sheep, is intended to provide constant stabilization of the dikes today. Additional polder areas where the Elbe can spread out during high water have been established recently.

The *furor hortensis* – as the victory of the landscape garden over its Baroque predecessors was called in England – that Prince Franz experienced during his many trips to England had already overtaken him as a young man. For the prince, as for the English aristocrats he visited at their great country estates, "a large domain, a meandering river and a forest" were soon counted among the absolute necessities of life, without which a gentleman could not cut a good figure with his lands. Just how completely Anhalt's ruler adopted an Anglophile lifestyle was demonstrated by his red "English" coat, in which he had his full-length portrait painted by the artist Anton von Maron, who was held in high esteem at the time. Probably the prince wanted this to be a signal to the beholder that for him these clothes not only were an elegant shell but also had a character-forming effect, suggestive of a certain way to behave. And that is how Prince Franz still stares down upon his life's work from the dining room wall of the Wörlitz Country House, in the company of his ancestors who have likewise been captured on canvas; he does not display the condescension befitting his rank, but rather appears to be inspired in some indeterminate manner, and one senses that his absorption could be directed either to the past or to the future.

Gärtnerhaus im Schlosspark Mosigkau
Gardener's house in the Mosigkau Palace park

Rokoko-Schloss Mosigkau, einst Sommerresidenz der Prinzessin Anna Wilhelmine von Anhalt-Dessau
Rococo palace of Mosigkau, formerly the summer residence of Princess Anna Wilhelmine of Anhalt-Dessau

»Ein Sommernachtstraum« am Nymphaeum in Wörlitz
"A Midsummer Night's Dream" at the Nymphaeum in Wörlitz

»Vulkanausbruch« auf der Insel »Stein«, Wörlitz
"Volcanic eruption" on Stone Island, Wörlitz

Blick auf Dessau, mit dem vorderen Tiergarten, dem Johannbau, St. Marien und Rathaus
View of Dessau with part of the zoo, Johannbau, St. Mary's Church and Town Hall

V.

The city of Dessau is undoubtedly the center (although not in a strict geographical sense) of the Garden Kingdom of Dessau-Wörlitz. Established close to where the Mulde flows into the Elbe, the former seat of the dukes of Anhalt-Dessau was officially renamed Dessau-Rosslau in 2008 in the course of the latest county reforms. Even today the city has not recovered from the terrible bombing attacks which almost completely destroyed it during the last two years of the Second World War. More than four decades of socialist city planning have likewise left their traces, and it is clear that the city will never recover its old glory. Historical transportation connections were intentionally negated, and the city was filled with unimaginative architectural pap made of standardized slabs.

The re-erection of the palace or other prominent historic buildings was avoided for programmatic reasons. "Obstructive ruins have to get out of the way," read the local news headlines for Dessau in the *Freiheit* from 22 May 1958.

"The purpose of historic preservation cannot be to preserve all such ruins without regard for usability, or even to return them to their former state. For instance, material and labor sufficient for constructing 120 apartments would have to be sacrificed in order to reconstruct the central section of the palace with the façade by Knobeldorff and the architecturally worthless entrance building. Moreover the palace hinders construction of an efficient connection to the bridge over the Mulde." The article ends with the sentence, "The path is free for the buildings of our socialist society."

In Folge der stalinistischen Stadtplanung zu Beginn des DDR-Regimes existiert heute nur noch der sogenannte Johannbau, kümmerlicher spätmittelalterlicher Rest eines einstmals eindrucksvollen Schlosskomplexes. Einsam und verlassen steht er im Umfeld unmalerischer, seit einiger Zeit auch ungenutzter Wohnblocks aus der Nachkriegszeit und beherbergt heute das Stadtmuseum. Die über Generationen gewachsene Vertrautheit der Bewohner mit ihrer gebauten Umgebung scheint auf merk-

As a result of Stalinist city planning at the beginning of the German Democratic Republic's regime, only the so-called Johannbau still survives today – a meager medieval remnant of a once impressive palace complex. Now housing the city museum, the building stands solitary and forlorn, in the vicinity of unattractive – and now unoccupied – apartment blocks from the post-war era. The intimacy between the townspeople and their built environment, which had evolved over generations, now

würdige Weise verloren gegangen zu sein. Hinzu kommt, dass die vierspurige Mulduferrandstraße die Stadt vom Fluss abschneidet und der westlich direkt daran angrenzende Tiergarten, ehemals herzogliches Jagdrevier und später Teil einer einst sehr geschätzten Auenlandschaft, ist nur über Umwege zu erreichen.

Darüber hinaus sind die Auswirkungen eines tiefgreifenden demografischen Wandels auf die urbane Entwicklung nach dem Zusammenbruch des DDR-Systems mit Wohnungsleerstand und dem daraus resultierenden Abriss ganzer Stadtviertel in den zwei zurückliegenden Jahrzehnten auch für den des Ortes Unkundigen allerorten sichtbar. Aus dem gerne als »Schrumpfung« bezeichneten Prozess sollen sich allerdings Chancen in der Konzentration auf spezifische städtische Potentiale entwickeln. Mit Hilfe des im Rahmen der Internationalen Bauausstellung 2010 entwickelten städtebaulichen Projekts »urbaner Kerne und landschaftlicher Zonen« möchte man das historische Gartenreich noch offensichtlicher in die Stadt Dessau einbeziehen; dies mittels sogenannter Pixel oder Claims, innerstädtische Landschaftsstücke, auf denen Bürger ihr Wohnumfeld individuell gestalten können. Ob mit der Schaffung wertvollen ökologischen Lebensraums Abwanderung verhindert und ein nachhaltiger sozioökonomischer Wandel eingeleitet werden kann, bleibt zu hoffen.

Apropos: Wie auch immer man die an den Hauptzufahrtsstraßen aufgestellten bunten Schilder mit dem Motto *An Dessau kommt keiner vorbei* interpretieren mag, in jedem Fall werden eher die üblichen braunen Hinweisschilder hilfreich sein, um die beiden mit dem Prädikat der UNESCO geadelten Welterbestätten sowie das ebenfalls ausgezeichnete, gebietsübergreifende Biosphärenreservat Mittelelbe zu entdecken.

seems strangely lost. In addition, a four-lane road along the Mulde riverbank cuts the city off from the river, and the zoo to the immediate west, formerly the dukes' hunting ground and later part of a once-appreciated floodplain, is only accessible via a roundabout route.

Furthermore, the impact of radical demographic changes on urban development after the collapse of the GDR system – manifested in empty apartments and the resulting demolition of entire city quarters over the past two decades – is also visible everywhere, even to those unfamiliar with the city. However, this process of "shrinking," as it is often called, also ought to offer an opportunity to concentrate on specific urban potentials. With the help of the city planning project "Urban Cores and Landscape Zones," developed within the framework of the International Building Exhibition for 2010, the historic Garden Kingdom is to be more clearly integrated into the city of Dessau; this is to be accomplished by means of so-called claims, sites within the inner-city landscape where citizens can individually design their surroundings. It remains to be seen whether the creation of valuable ecological living space will prevent urban emigration and if it will be possible to introduce sustainable socio-economic change.

Apropos: however the colorful signs on the main approaches to the city with the motto *An Dessau kommt keiner vorbei* (You can't bypass Dessau) are interpreted, it is the traditional brown signs that will be more helpful for the many visitors who come to discover the two sites with the UNESCO World Heritage titles and the likewise outstanding trans-regional Middle Elbe Biosphere Reserve.

Ruinenbrücke im Landschaftspark Georgium
So-called Bridge of Ruins in Georgium

Cover: *Villa Hamilton*
Seite 1: *Deckenmalerei im Floratempel, Wörlitz*
Seite 2: *Eisenhart in Wörlitz*
Karte: Kulturstiftung DessauWörlitz /
Team VIERZIG A, Dresden

Die Deutsche Nationalbibliothek verzeichnet diese Publikation in der Deutschen Nationalbibliografie; detaillierte bibliografische Daten sind im Internet über http://dnb.ddb.de abrufbar.

© Hinstorff Verlag GmbH, Rostock 2010
Lagerstraße 7, 18055 Rostock
Tel. 0381 / 4969-0
www.hinstorff.de
www.edition-rk.com

Alle Rechte vorbehalten. Reproduktionen, Speicherungen in Datenverarbeitungsanlagen, Wiedergabe auf fotomechanischen, elektronischen oder ähnlichen Wegen, Vortrag und Funk – auch auszugsweise – nur mit Genehmigung des Verlages.

1. Auflage 2010
Herstellung: Hinstorff Verlag GmbH
Lektor: Dr. Florian Ostrop
Druck und Bindung: Himmer AG
Printed in Germany
ISBN: 978-3-356-01362-7

Front cover: Villa Hamilton
Page 1: Ceiling painting in the Flora Temple, Wörlitz
Page 2: Eisenhart, partly built of bog ore, in Wörlitz
Map: DessauWörlitz Cultural Foundation /
Team VIERZIG A, Dresden

The Deutsche Bibliothek lists this publication in the Deutsche Nationalbibliografie; detailed bibliographic data can be found on the internet at http//dnb.ddb.de

© Hinstorff Verlag GmbH, Rostock 2010
Lagerstraße 7, 18055 Rostock
Tel. 0381 / 4969-0
www.hinstorff.de
www.edition-rk.com

All rights reserved. No part of this publication, including excerpts, can be reproduced, stored on computer, disseminated through photocopies or by electronic or other means, used in lectures, on the radio, etc. without permission of the publisher.

First edition 2010
Production: Hinstorff Verlag GmbH
Editor: Dr. Florian Ostrop
Printing and Binding: Himmer AG
Printed in Germany
ISBN: 978-3-356-01362-7

*Gewitterstimmung über dem Barockschloss Oranienbaum,
dessen Stil und Name auf die Fürstin Henriette Catharina, eine geborene Prinzessin von Oranien-Nassau, zurückgeht*
Approaching storm at the Baroque palace of Oranienbaum, whose name refers to Princess Henriette Catharina, née Oranien-Nassau

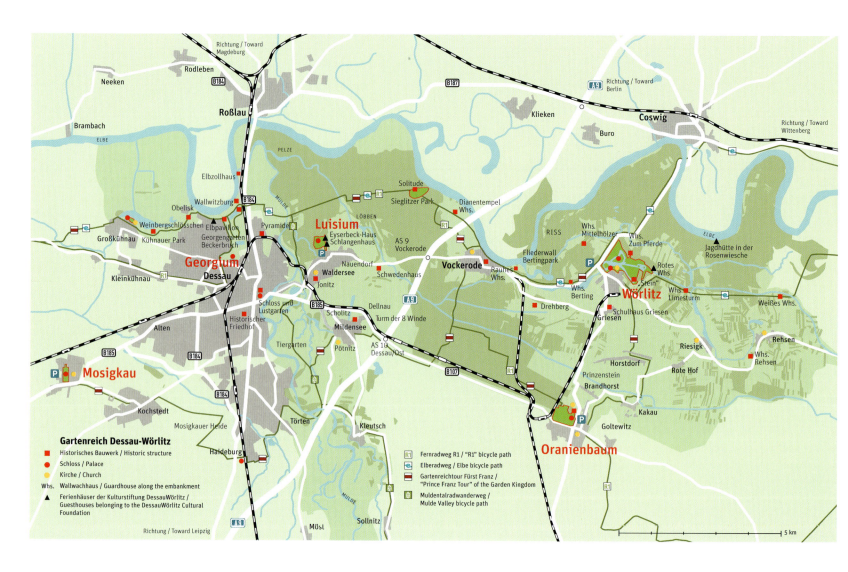